FREDERICK DOUGLASS AND THE NORTH STAR

LORENZO PACE

WINDMILL BOOKS

New York

Published in 2015 by The Rosen Publishing Group, Inc.
29 East 21st Street, New York, NY 10010

First Edition

Book Design: Brian Garvey

Illustrator: Lorenzo Pace

Library of Congress Cataloging-in-Publication Data

Pace, Lorenzo.
Frederick Douglass and the North Star / by Lorenzo Pace.
p. cm. — (African American quartet)
ISBN 978-1-4777-9281-0 (library binding) — ISBN 978-1-4777-9282-7 (pbk.) — ISBN 978-1-4777-9283-4 (6-pack)
1. Douglass, Frederick, 1818–1895 — Juvenile literature. 2. Abolitionists — United States — Juvenile literature. 3. African American abolitionists — Juvenile literature. 4. Antislavery movements — United States — History — 19th century — Juvenile literature. I. Pace, Lorenzo. II. Title.
E449.D75 P334 2015
973.8—d23

Manufactured in the United States of America

All artwork by Lorenzo Pace.
Cover photo SuperStock/Getty Images, p. 47 Cindy Reiman.

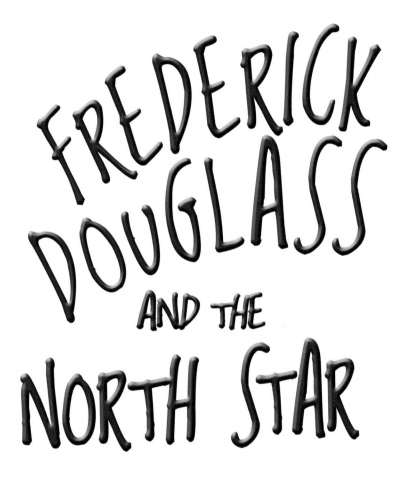

This book is about slavery and the brave people who fought against it. More than three hundred years ago, some people in Africa were sold into slavery.

Fig. 226. Slave transport in Africa

5

These African slaves traveled to the United States in sailing ships. They were packed in tightly under horrible conditions. Many died during the voyage.

7

Many people did not believe that one person should own another. These people protested. They were abolitionists. They wanted to abolish slavery.

But slavery continued because many landowners, especially in the Southern states of the United States, made money from others' work. These people needed slaves to work in the fields.

Throughout the Southern states, there were slave markets where people were bought and sold.

Some slaves managed to escape to freedom. One heroic former slave who dedicated his life to help free his brothers and sisters was Frederick Douglass.

15

He wrote a book about
his life as a slave. Many
people read his book
and were moved by
what he had to say.
They, too, wanted to join
him to end slavery.

17

Many joined the struggle,
including the former
slave Harriet Tubman.
She worked on the
Underground Railroad,
and helped slaves to
freedom in the North.

18

The Underground Railroad was a network of secret routes that helped slaves travel to the North and to freedom. Many people risked their lives to help the slaves avoid capture.

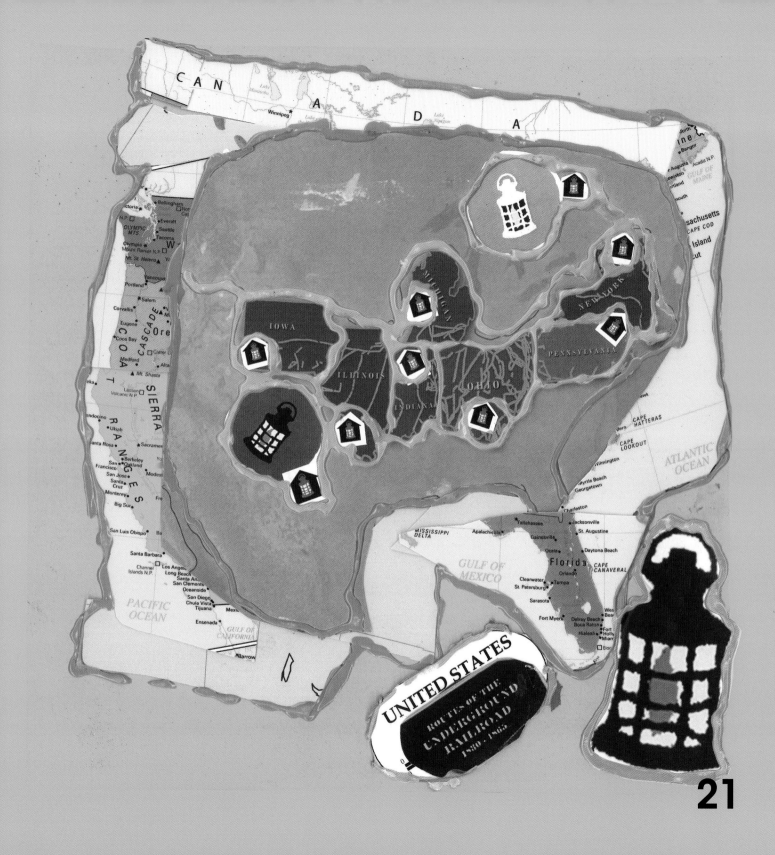

UNITED STATES

ROUTES OF THE UNDERGROUND RAILROAD 1830-1865

21

William Garrison was never a slave, but he was one of the men who helped with the struggle. He worked with Frederick Douglass to make a newspaper: *The North Star*. This newspaper told people about slavery.

23

Frederick Douglass wrote for *The North Star*. He was an excellent writer and he convinced many people with his words.

FREDERICK DOUGLASS

"It is easier to build strong children than to repair broken men."

25

Frederick Douglass
not only wrote strongly
against slavery, he also
spoke in front of many
people. He spoke often
at the African Church
in Rochester, New York,
where he lived.

AFRICAN CHURCH
ROCHESTER, NY.

AFRICAN CHURCH
ROCHESTER, NY.

27

The slave owners fought back. They did not want their slaves to be free. They thought of these people as their property. When a slave escaped, the owners put advertisements in the newspaper and offered rewards.

run away slave

Slaves—Slaves.
The subscriber has just received and of-
fers for sale at his old stand, No. 7 Moreau
street, Third Municipality, New Orleans,
the largest lot of NEGROES in the city,
consisting of house servants, field hands,
and mechanics. They will be sold on reasonable terms for
cash or good paper.   WM. F. TALBOTT

TWENTY FIVE DOLLARS REWARD—Will
be paid for the apprehension of the mulatto boy
DANIEL, aged about twenty three years and about
five feet five inches high. He left his master's plantation in Iberville on the evening of the 4th in t
and came to this city on the steamboat E. D. White. The
above reward will be paid for his delivery at the parish
jail, or to   W. M. GREENWOOD,
                   10 Old Levee street

TWENTY FIVE DOLLARS REWARD—Ran
away in the early part of February the negro man
RINGGOLD. He is about 34 years old, about 6
feet 3 or 4 inches high is a griff, can speak a little
French, is a carpenter, whitewasher &c. The
public are cautioned against employing or harboring said
boy. Any person delivering the said boy to me at McDon-
oghville, shall receive the above reward
                   CHARLES KORNER

TEN DOLLARS REWARD—Ran away on the
5th January, my negro woman ROSETTA, black
36 years of age, 5 feet 4 or 5 inches high. She be-
longs to the estate of Mr. Isaac Pipkin, deceased,
I will give the above reward to any one who will
apprehend and deliver her up at Warwick & Martin's trad-
ing yard, Common street.
        W. B. MUSE, agent for the heirs.

TWENTY DOLLARS REWARD—Ran away
on the 6th inst. from the plantation of A. Arm-
strong, on Bayou Lafourche, the negro man JOE
about 44 years of age, 5 feet 6 inches high, dark
griffe very stout and broad shouldered, heavy dull
manner and a husky voice when speaking, has a sore on his
left shin bone not yet quite well. He will probably be
found about the steamboats having been hired by his
master owner, Capt. P. Kirney, as a fireman on the tow-
boats. We will give the above reward to any one arr-
esting and putting him in jail, not take wages of the em-
ployer.   CAUMACK & SQUI...

29

Frederick Douglass never stopped fighting for justice. His courage was recognized by many people. The president of the United States, Abraham Lincoln, even invited Frederick Douglass to the White House.

Abraham Lincoln believed that The United States should be a country that did not have slaves. Many people in the Southern states disagreed. The Northern states and the Southern states fought a civil war because of this disagreement. Many African American soldiers fought for the Northern states. Many died to end slavery. The Northern states won the war. Owning slaves was now against the law.

Frederick Douglass died on February 20, 1895. He lived to see slavery come to an end. His determination, hard work, and persuasive writing helped to make this happen.

FREDERICK DOUGLASS,
AMERICAN SLAVE.

"Once you learn to read, you will be forever free."

35

When I was a little boy
in Alabama, each room
of my two-room wooden
schoolhouse had a picture
of Frederick Douglass.
He was a hero to all the
teachers and students. Our
teachers taught us that to
learn to read and write was
our most important job.

37

Learning to read was a gift that some people were denied. Frederick Douglass was taught to read by the person who owned him.

"Once you learn to read, you will be forever free."

"Once you learn to read, you will be forever free."

39

The books that Frederick Douglass wrote made many people think about African Americans differently. Future generations were influenced by his powerful words about dignity and human rights for all people.

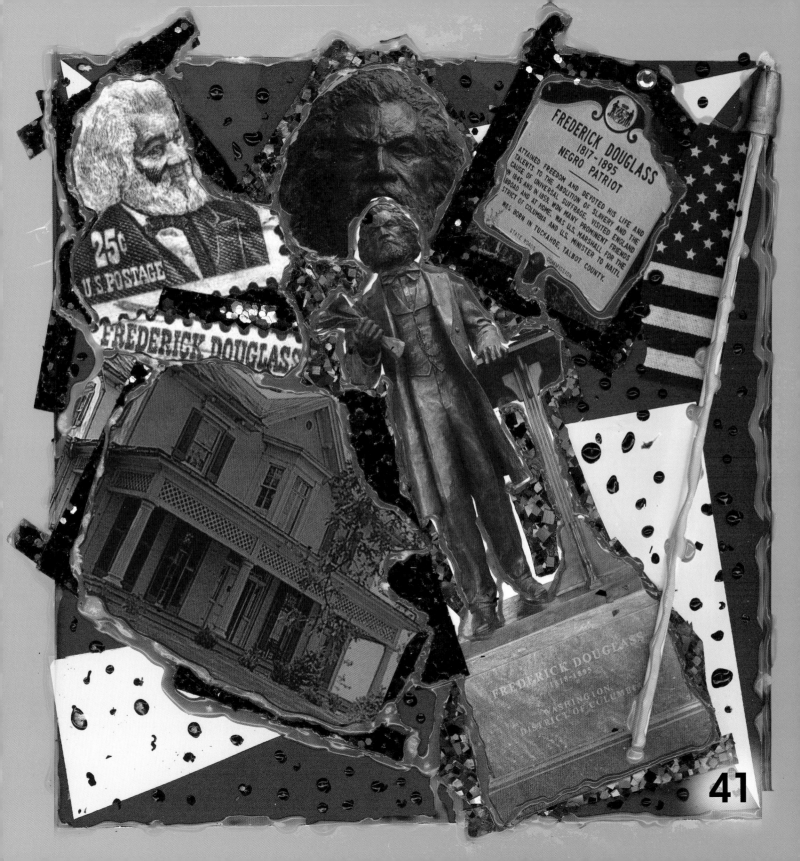

41

The leaders of the civil rights movement, such as Martin Luther King Jr., Booker T. Washington, George Washington Carver, and Claudette Colvin, all knew the words of Frederick Douglass. You can say that they were the children of his way of thinking.

I am a child of the thoughts of Frederick Douglass. All my life I collected his books and documents about his life. My sculpture "Triumph of the Human Spirit," in the heart of New York City, celebrates our African American ancestors. *The North Star* showed me the way.

Born in Birmingham, Alabama, Lorenzo Pace spent his adolescence in Chicago, Illinois. He received his BFA and MFA degrees from the School of the Art Institute of Chicago and his doctorate in art education and administration from Illinois State University in Normal, Illinois. Working with a diversity of objects and materials, Lorenzo has exhibited his sculpture and installations and presented his performance art both nationally and internationally.

In 1992, he was presented with the Keys to the City of Birmingham, Alabama, by Mayor Richard Arrington and Birmingham councilmen Leroy "Tuffy" Bandy and Bernard Kincaid. In 2000, Lorenzo's work was included in "Out of Action: Performance Art 1949–1999," an exhibition of the Museum of Contemporary Art, Tokyo. In the 2008 Olympics in Beijing, Lorenzo represented the United States in an exhibition entitled "One World One Dream" at the Sunshine International Museum of Contemporary Art.

In 2011, investigating his family roots in Tuskegee, Alabama, Lorenzo included as part of a permanent historical marker and art installation a bronze replica of the original slave lock that had held his great-grandfather captive. This installation is at the AME Zion Church in Creek Stand, Alabama, one of the oldest existing slave cemeteries in the United States.

In 2013, Lorenzo's work was also part of a site-specific art installation to honor those people who were taken as slaves from Buea, Cameroon. This installation was part of the "Festival of Sounds, Color, and Arts of Africa" in Douala, Cameroon.

In 2014, Lorenzo was invited to participate in "HistoryMakers," a video oral history of contemporary artists, writers, musicians, actors, and dancers that is now part of the permanent collection at the Library of Congress in Washington, D.C.

Lorenzo currently maintains a studio in Brooklyn, New York. He is the sculptor commissioned to create "Triumph of the Human Spirit" for the African Burial Ground Memorial in Foley Square Park in New York City. He is currently a professor of art at the University of Texas–Rio Grande Valley.

Acknowledgments

The last twenty-five years of continuous personal research of my family tree has been a daunting task, but the end result was to find my family's roots. These books are a major part of this ongoing search, and they are dedicated to many family members and friends. Starting with members of the Clark family who are present today: to Uncle Willie Clark Jr. (1909), Aunt Evelyn Clark (1929), and Elnora Clark Peewee (1914) in Birmingham, Alabama. To members who have passed in the Pace family: my resolute uncle Julian Pace (1911–2006), who presented the original slave lock to me, and to my mother Mary A. Pace (1916–1993) and father Bishop Elder Eddie T. Pace (1909–1991).

These books are also dedicated to my children: Shawn, Ezra, Jalani (the namesake for the first book), and Esperanza. Much respect and thanks to my cousin Shari Williams, director of the Ridge Project of Tuskegee, Alabama, for taking on the difficult task of researching my family tree, starting in Creek Stand, Alabama, the original place of the slave lock of Steve Pace. To all my friends and colleagues who encouraged me to keep going and not to give up on my quest to better understand our collective humanity.

To my little brother Ronald Pace, who is an author himself (*Cane Is Able*, 2012), for his invaluable suggestions and support, which enabled these books to come alive. To the great artist, printmaker, and musician Jose William, who gave me my first art exhibition at the South Side Art Center in Chicago and helped me make my first silk-screen quilt print. To my old Chicago friend and entrepreneur Walter Patrick, who in 1989 first suggested that the publishers review the prototype for *Jalani and the Lock*. Without this introduction, the book might not have come to fruition.

To my colleague Professor Leila Hernandez, an excellent graphic designer at the University of Texas–Rio Grande Valley, for her suggestion to use my grandmother's and mother's quilts as part of the visual concept of the Harriet Tubman volume. To Chicago impresario and author Tom Burrell (*Brainwashed*, 2004), who believed in me before I believed in myself, praising my early artwork and collecting it to this day. To Cassandra Griffen, photojournalist, for her gracious contribution in allowing me to use her photograph of Birmingham civil rights icon Fred Shuttlesworth.

To my soul mate, former teacher at the School of the Art Institute of Chicago, and author Ronne Hartfield (*Another Way Home*, 2004), who introduced me to African literature and heritage as a young art student. This self-reflection led me to the African symbol "Sankofa" meaning "in order to understand oneself as a person, you must look back at your past to move forward into the future." Therefore, to start this process, I had to go to the Motherland of all humanity, Africa.

All this could not have happened without the help, support, and understanding of one of my dearest friends, Lamine Gueye, and his very special family in Dakar, Senegal, West Africa. My travels there to one of Africa's largest slave castles in Gorée Island have provided me with invaluable information and research on the early slave trade to the Americas.

To the publisher Roger Rosen, who had the courage and vision to tackle some of America's most sensitive topics. His orchestration and sensitivity to the completion of these books have made me keenly aware of what a privilege it was to collaborate with this forward-thinking human being. To Brian Garvey, a wonderful graphic designer who was completely up to the challenge of creatively manipulating the visual concepts of the books. Finally, to my brothers and sisters in the Pace family: Eddie Jr., Lawrence, Michael, Alfonzo, William, Ronald, Dorothy, Mary, Shirley, and my sweet sister-in-law Yvonne. To all our future children and to the visionaries who believe in the essence of humanity, so that we can all live in peace and love, celebrating our differences on this beautiful planet that we all share.

~ Dr. Lorenzo Pace

ULTIMATE TRAINS

WRITTEN BY **Peter McMahon**
ILLUSTRATED BY **Andy Mora**

Kids Can Press

To my sweet wife, Kristina, and to John Stevens, the best editor a grandson could have over the years — P.M.

Acknowledgments

Thanks first-and-foremost to Karen Li for her editing goodness and a wonderful creative collaboration on this book. Thanks also to my good friend David Howard, whose ideas, shop class and decades of imaginative know-how were pivotal in getting the models in this book to come to life. Finally, thanks to the folks at the EfstonScience store in Toronto, Ontario, for their advice and for providing the materials to create the experiments in this book.

Text © 2010 Peter McMahon
Illustrations © 2010 Andy Mora

Kids Can Press acknowledges the financial support of the Government of Ontario, through the Ontario Media Development Corporation's Ontario Book Initiative; the Ontario Arts Council; the Canada Council for the Arts; and the Government of Canada, through the BPIDP, for our publishing activity.

Published in Canada by
Kids Can Press Ltd.
29 Birch Avenue
Toronto, ON M4V 1E2

Published in the U.S. by
Kids Can Press Ltd.
2250 Military Road
Tonawanda, NY 14150

www.kidscanpress.com

Edited by Karen Li
Designed by Kathleen Gray

This book is smyth sewn casebound.
Manufactured in Singapore, in 4/2010 by Tien Wah Press (Pte) Ltd.

CM 10 0 9 8 7 6 5 4 3 2 1

Library and Archives Canada Cataloguing in Publication

McMahon, Peter, 1977–
   Ultimate trains / written by Peter McMahon; illustrated by Andy Mora.

(Machines of the future)
Includes index.
ISBN 978-1-55453-366-4

1. Railroad trains — Juvenile literature. 2. High speed trains — Juvenile literature. 3. Magnetic levitation vehicles — Juvenile literature. I. Mora, Andy II. Title. III. Series: Machines of the future

TF148.M34 2010   j385   C2010-900441-8

Kids Can Press is a *Corus*™ Entertainment company

Contents

TH JOURNEY GINS

Imagine it's 100 years ago, and you're about to take a trip. Most likely, you're waiting at a train station. The whistle blows. The conductor shouts, "All aboard!" You step on with your bags, and you're off!

Trees sail by faster than if you were on horseback. Lakes and rivers appear almost instantly. If you're traveling on an "express" train, you'll be cruising along at approximately 65 km/h (40 m.p.h.). At that speed, whole cities pass by about as fast as they would if you were traveling in the latest form of transportation: the automobile. A hundred years ago, trains were the fastest form of mass transportation on Earth. Ships could take weeks to make their journeys. Cars had only been in production for a handful of years. When it came to getting around at top speed and in style, trains were king.

With names such as America's Sunset Limited, the Texas Special and the Canadian Continental, these steel workhorses took travelers on grand adventures well into the early years of highways and air travel.

Now … pretend it's ten years from today. Again, you're waiting to travel. You could be driving or taking a plane, but just as likely, you'll be waiting to board a train. Even in this age of eco-jets and hybrid cars, trains are the way of the future … again.

Your share of the energy needed to propel a train creates less pollution than traveling by a car or plane: Trains are the world's only kind of mass transportation that can run partially or totally on electricity. High-speed trains can move people quickly between cities, countries and — someday perhaps — even continents.

A note on safety

The activities described in this book have many steps, but the results are worth the effort. For safety, enlist an adult's help to build each experiment. Be sure to wear protective eyewear whenever cutting or drilling into heavy material. And when it comes to using power tools, be smart: Let your friendly neighborhood adult do the work while you supervise!

Traveling hundreds of kilometers (miles) an hour on computer-controlled tracks, these trains use electricity, gas turbines and even magnets to top out at close to half the speed of sound.

Want to see for yourself? Join the people who are building the trains of tomorrow for a high-speed tour of the next generation of transportation. Build your own locomotive engine, high-powered electromagnets and a levitating bullet train. Think you have what it takes to be a conductor on the rails of the future? All aboard!

ON THE RIGHT TRACK ... FOR 5000 YEARS

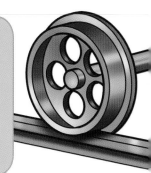

The oldest known wheel was discovered in 2003 by archaeologists in Slovenia. It dates back to 3000 BCE.

The late 1700s saw the invention of flanges, the part on modern train wheels that hangs over the rails to keep the wheels from slipping off the track. Also, iron had replaced wood as the prime material for building rails.

As early as 1550, "wagonways" (roads incorporating lengths of wood) were used in Germany to move heavy loads. It was easier for horse-drawn wagons and carts to move over these primitive railway tracks than over loose dirt or mud.

By the first century CE, one of the main streets in the ancient city of Pompeii was heavily grooved from use. The deeper the grooves, the easier it was for simple carts and wagons to follow the road. Could these be considered the first tracks?

Around 1800, British inventor Richard Trevithick created the first steam engine small enough to be used in a vehicle. In February 1804, a mighty locomotive successfully pulled 10 tonnes (11 tons) of iron and 70 people 15 km (9 mi.) through Wales … in two hours.

In Northern England, George Stephenson constructed the first efficient passenger locomotive in 1825. It traveled 15 km (9 mi.) in only one hour! More impressively, it could do so while hauling 450 passengers in more than 20 cars.

The "Pullman sleeper" was invented by American George Pullman around 1857. It was designed for comfortable overnight passenger travel. (Wireless Internet in your bunk was still a few years off …)

The last spike of the Canadian Pacific Railway (CPR) was driven into the ground in 1885 at Craigellachie, British Columbia. After a year of final touches, the CPR opened as the first link from Canada's East Coast to the West. At the time, it was also the world's longest railroad.

STEAM POWER: MASS TRANSIT IS BORN!

The late eighteenth century marked the beginning of the first Industrial Revolution. In parts of Europe and later in North America, this was the greatest explosion of new technology the world had ever seen. During this time, steam power largely replaced muscle power (which usually meant the muscles of horses). Not only did steam begin to move trains, it also powered furnaces and pumps that drained water from mines.

Early locomotives harnessed steam power by burning coal to heat water-filled tubes, converting the water to steam. The steam blasted into cylinders with movable parts, called pistons. The steam expanded and so pushed the pistons. This action drove the rods and cranks that moved the wheels of the train.

Exhaust steam

Steam

Water-filled tubes

Coal-burning furnace

Cylinder   Piston   Piston rod

Project #1: STEAM ENGINE IN A SALAD BOWL

Believe it or not, you can make your own basic steam engine in less than an hour using a small number of household items and hardware store parts. Thin copper tubing is available at most science hobby stores. It can easily snap, so you may want to buy extra lengths.

YOU WILL NEED

an empty, dry soda pop can

masking tape

heavy-duty scissors

30 cm (12 in.) or longer of 0.25 cm (1/8 in.) copper tubing

highlighter or other fat marker

metal file

pliers with wire cutters

a tea light candle

modeling clay

a large bowl (at least four times as wide as the soda pop can)

matches

Expert interview

"Compared to modern diesel locomotives of today, steam engines were loud, messy and high maintenance. But there's something about the movement of the pistons and rods attached to the wheels ... the rhythmic chug-chug-chug of these mighty machines. It was definitely the most interesting way to get around. Think of these old locomotives while you build your own basic steam engine starting on the next page."
— longtime Canadian National Railway conductor Marvin Harvey

INSTRUCTIONS

1 Cut off the top two-thirds of the soda pop can with a pair of scissors and tape over the sharp edges. Before setting it aside, press on the inside bottom of the can until the little dent in the middle is flat.

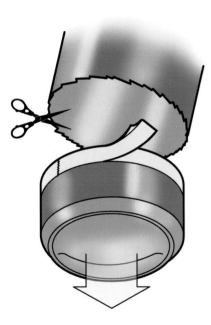

2 Firmly hold the copper tubing and, beginning in the middle, carefully wind the tubing around the fat marker three times. Remove the marker.

3 Bend each end of copper tubing down and out to the left. If it looks like your coiled copper tubing will hang out of the soda pop can by more than 2.5 cm (1 in.) on each side, cut off the excess on each end with wire cutters. File off the rough edges.

4 Poke two holes opposite each other on the sides of the can near the base. Carefully thread each end of the copper tube assembly through one of the two holes. The coil should sit just above the center of the can. Be sure there is the same amount of copper tubing on both sides of the coil so as not to affect your engine's balance.

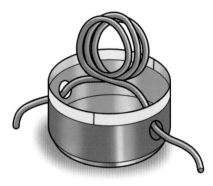

5 Place the candle inside the can. The wick should just about touch the coiled tubing. Seal the holes around the tubing with modeling clay to keep water out. Add more as needed to keep the candle centered and to balance your steam engine.

6 Fill the salad bowl with water. Then carefully hold the soda pop can and contents so that one end of the tubing is under the tap. Fill the tubing with water, then stop both ends with your fingers and set the entire thing in the bowl. Once both ends of the copper tubing are underwater, gently let go.

7 Light the candle and wait for the water in the coil to heat up. After a few moments, you'll see this steam-powered assembly start to spin as the hot water in the coiled tube expands, blows out of the tube ends and sets the engine in motion.

DIESEL POWER: TRAINS GET STRONG

Though steam locomotives continued to dominate the transportation scene well into the twentieth century, they were not energy efficient. In early engines, only about 10 percent of the energy released from burning coal actually helped move the train forward; the other 90 percent was wasted as heat.

To increase energy efficiency, refrigerator engineer Rudolph Diesel created and refined the locomotive engine that would bear his name by the beginning of the twentieth century. Diesel engines would eventually be able to translate more power to the wheels than steam engines, most usefully when accelerating the train from a stand still.

Diesel locomotive engines don't need to burn coal or boil water. They work by compressing air in cylinders until it is very hot. The air then ignites fuel that is sprayed into the cylinders. The explosion pushes the piston, creating power and moving the train wheels.

Diesel fuel

Exhaust

Air

Hot compressed air

Cylinder

Explosion

Piston

Piston rod

By the mid-1920s, improvements to diesel locomotives made them cleaner and more powerful than steam locomotives. Their energy efficiency climbed to more than 40 percent. By the 1950s, railroad companies around the world began to switch from steam engines to diesel.

In the 1970s, the old diesel engines were further improved to become diesel-electric trains: A diesel-electric engine drives electric turbines. The turbines then power the train's wheels. In theory, modern diesel-electric engines could be as much as 75 percent energy efficient!

Electric trains — which had been under development since the 1890s — also came into widespread use during the mid-1900s. For the most part, electric trains work best within city limits because they are powered by electric rails or overhead wires. We enjoy such technology most often underneath many of the world's biggest cities … as subways.

GREEN POWER: TRAINS GET SMART

The push for energy efficiency has made train travel cheaper (less fuel is needed to power the engine) ... and greener. From cleaner diesel engines to biofuel-powered locomotives to electric monorails, many of today's trains let you travel in style while being kind to the Earth. In fact, a trip on an electric or high-efficiency diesel-fueled train can be two to six times friendlier to the environment than other forms of transportation. When it comes to ozone-harming carbon-dioxide (CO_2) emissions, trains are the greenest way to travel over medium and long distances.

While the U.S. has lagged behind many Asian and European countries in developing modern railways to travel from city to city, some states have plans to catch up: In 2010, California got funding to build a high-speed electric rail line between San Francisco and Los Angeles. According to plans, the 350 km/h (218 m.p.h.) train will be similar to models in Japan and parts of Europe. This model will reduce the need for oil by more than 12 million barrels a year.

As well, some U.S. rail lines recently began using 25 percent biodiesel in traditional diesel locomotives. Biodiesel is an alternative fuel made from renewable sources, like leftover cooking grease, animal fat or plant oils. It can be used on its own or blended with regular diesel.

What's great is that many of the routes fueled by biodiesel blends are used for transporting grains. Just imagine: a grain-fueled train used to deliver grain!

What's your greenest ride?

	AIRPLANE	AUTOMOBILE	TRAIN
Pollution (including CO_2) per passenger, per km (3/5 mi.)	494 g (17 oz.)	271 g (10 oz.)	85 g (3 oz.)

(source: adapted from Sierra Club)

THE QUEST TO SPEED

With the arrival of cheap, mass transit by rail in the 1960s and '70s, something else began to grip the imaginations of engineers: speed. The quest to be fastest was exciting, but being able to quickly move lots of people around also promised riches for the companies that could safely pull it off.

By the 1970s, electric, gas turbine and even hovercraft-based trains had reached top speeds of between 300 and 400 km/h (186–249 m.p.h.). These futuristic trains featured long, straight tracks, high-powered electric motors and oversized wheels.

They also took advantage of new technologies. For example, France's TGV (Train à Grande Vitesse, or high-speed train), has in-train signaling: Drivers no longer need to slow down enough to see the signals by the side of the tracks.

That same decade, a new technology started to approach — and then broke — all speed records: Magnetic levitation trains, or maglevs, used ultra powerful electromagnets to lift and propel rail cars. By 1980, maglevs had reached speeds of more than 500 km/h (311 m.p.h.). In 2003, an experimental maglev in Japan clocked in at an eyelid-flapping 581 km/h (361 m.p.h.) That's about twice the speed of a jetliner during takeoff.

Faster than a speeding ...

The Shinkansen — Japan's bullet train — carried its five-billionth passenger in 2000. France's two-billionth passenger mark is expected to be reached in 2010 by its TGV system.

At the throttle controls

Just think what you could do at the controls of the world's most extreme trains: One is so slow you could run beside it on foot. Another can travel as fast as a passenger plane. Without a doubt, sitting up-front on one of these rides would be the experience of a lifetime.

• The slowest train on Earth is also the only running train in Cambodia. Because of its 17 km/h (10 m.p.h.) top speed, passengers who can't fit inside with cargo can ride on the roof.

• In December 2009, China's *Harmony* express train set the record for the fastest long-distance rail trip, traveling 1100 km (684 mi.) from the southern city of Guangzhou to the central city of Wuhan in less than three hours! Top speed: 350 km/h (217 m.p.h.).

• Old Dominion University in Virginia was supposed to have a small maglev to whisk students around campus by 2002, but project coordinators are still waiting to flip on the switch. Top speed? Low 10s of km/h (6 to 10 m.p.h.).

• In 2003, at Holloman Air Force Base (New Mexico, U.S.), an unmanned rocket sled screamed down a multi-kilometer-long railway at a speed that is unlikely to be beat on any commuter rail anytime soon: 10 430 km/h (6481 m.p.h.). In fighter-pilot lingo, that's Mach 8.5 — about half the speed of a spaceship in orbit.

• France's TGV currently holds the world speed record for conventional rail trains. In April 2007, a modified TGV reached a speed of 575 km/h (357 m.p.h.) under test-track conditions.

Project #2: RIDING THE RAILS

You can drive a car without a road and you can land a plane without a runway, but to run a train, the first thing you need is tracks. Tracks decide where a train can go, how fast it can travel and how much weight it can carry. Copy the templates on the next page to see how tracks affect your journey on the rails.

YOU WILL NEED

track templates (see page 21)

train template (see page 20)

20 cm x 25 cm (8 in. x 10 in.) printer-friendly card stock

scissors

tape

Expert interview

"In building the cardboard tracks described in the next few pages, you'll get a sense for how certain trains on certain tracks can go certain speeds. Freight trains, for example, are assigned a certain speed limit. When approaching a stop or changing to a different track, trains have to go at a specific lower speed. Push your train quickly around the curves in your model tracks and you'll see why."

— longtime Canadian National Railway conductor Marvin Harvey

INSTRUCTIONS

1 Scan the train template on this page into your computer. Print the template on printer-friendly card stock and cut it out. If you are using a photocopier, copy the page and cut out the template. Trace it onto card stock and cut it out.

2 Fold template along the dotted lines in the direction indicated by arrows. Match the symbols $\oplus \oplus$ and $\ominus \ominus$, and attach them with tape.

3 Fold down the sides of your train so that they will hug the rails of your track.

4 Repeat Steps 1 and 2 for the track templates on the opposite page. The track templates can be arranged and taped into an infinite number of track designs.

Train-building tip

Once you have planned your track design, print or copy two or three of these pages, cut out the templates you need and copy those onto one page. Then you can copy that page as many times as you need without wasting pages of tracks you won't use. When you're finished, either recycle all the card stock or proudly display your track system around your home.

train

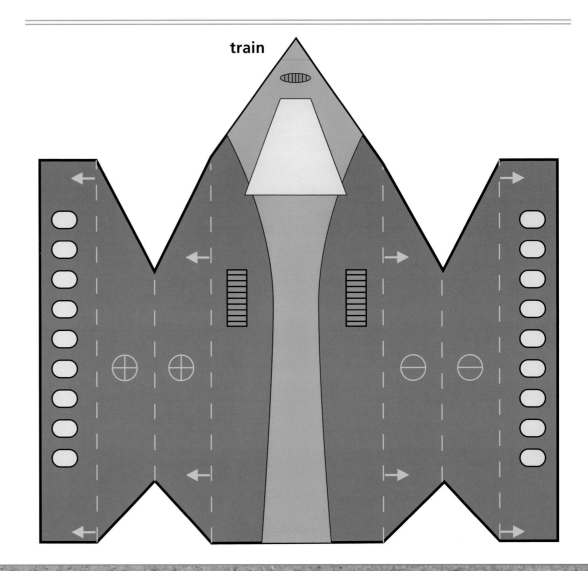

5 Run the train on the tracks and see how tight you can make the turns before the train goes off track. Can your train make the curve if it goes slower? How do steep hills affect speed?

Today's trains often use the same tracks that have been in place for decades. Dual metal rails are kept the right distance apart by spikes driven through sleepers (the lengths of wood you see every few feet on tracks) into the ground. Trains "steer" around obstacles or oncoming trains by using switches and signals to change course to a different set of tracks.

Though rails on the first tracks were made of iron, modern rails are made of steel alloy. Higher quality rail steel allows trains to run faster and carry more weight.

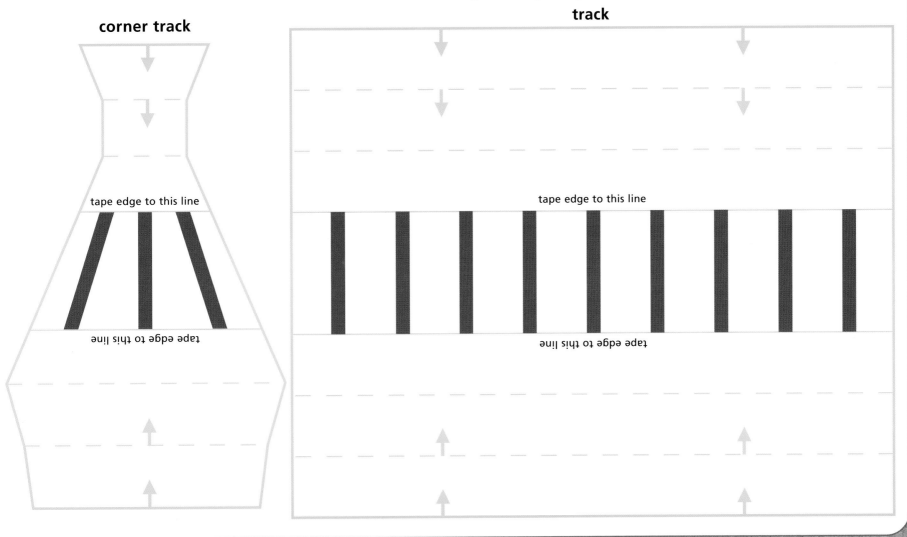

corner track

tape edge to this line

tape edge to this line

track

tape edge to this line

tape edge to this line

Faster than cars and cheaper than airplanes, maglev trains could someday whisk people between cities and maybe even continents. These electromagnet-powered vehicles are not only fast and efficient, they're also some of the greenest on the planet. Maglevs make little air pollution in terms of exhaust (they have no exhaust), and they also don't require as much maintenance.

Unlike conventional trains, which use engines that run on fossil fuels, maglev trains don't have "engines." In many cases, the maglev tracks drive the train. Many maglev tracks work by creating electromagnetic fields. One electromagnetic field allows a train to float above its tracks. Another field constantly changes to alternately push and pull the train forward.

Using magnetism to move vehicles is both easy and hard: Easy, because the universe has plenty of magnetism (and magnetism waiting to happen). Hard, because creating magnetism is one thing — harnessing it is another.

Magnets in spaaaace ...

The biggest magnetic field in our cosmic backyard is right on top of us: Earth's magnetic poles are located just off of the geographic North Pole and South Pole. When you watch a compass point north, you're seeing the compass needle (a tiny magnet free to move on a pivot) attracted to Earth's magnetic north. (If you were standing at the North Pole, your compass needle would spin around in circles.)

You can see a small magnetic field in action using a common bar magnet. Sprinkle very small, fine pieces of metal — iron filings, for example — on a piece of paper, and hold your magnet underneath. Tap the paper until the filings shuffle around to make an "image" of your handy portable magnetic field.

What you're seeing is magnetic lines of force flowing from the north pole of the magnet to the south, attracting metals at one end and repelling them at the other. "Like" parts of different magnets (north-north or south-south) repel each other, while — as they say — opposites attract.

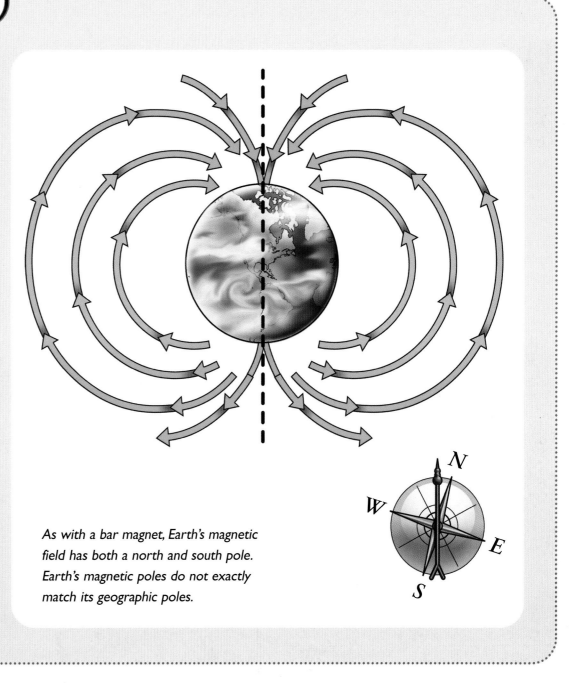

As with a bar magnet, Earth's magnetic field has both a north and south pole. Earth's magnetic poles do not exactly match its geographic poles.

TU NING UP T E JUICE

Maglev trains usually use electromagnets, not just permanent magnets like the ones you find in everyday life. Unlike naturally occurring magnets that always attract or repel, electromagnets exert a magnetic field only when "excited" by having an electric current run through them.

A weak electromagnet can be created by connecting one end of a wire to the positive end of a household D-cell battery, and then connecting the other end of the wire to the negative end of the battery.

Here's how it all works: Inside a battery case, electrons tend to collect at one end (the negative, or "–", terminal). Wire a battery's terminals to a gadget that requires electricity, such as a lightbulb, and the gadget will receive power as electrons are pulled from the battery's negative terminal to the gadget's positive (or "+") terminal.

So what happens when you connect the ends of a battery with a wire? Electrons will flow through the wire, from the battery's negative terminal to its positive terminal. This "excites" the wire and creates an electromagnetic field. Disconnect either end of the wire from the battery, and the magnetic field disappears.

PROJECT #3: MAKE YOUR OWN ELECTROMAGNET

In a way, electromagnets are all around your home. Gather the materials below to see how you can make and use your own. You can find varnish-insulated wire at large electronics stores or science hobby stores.

YOU WILL NEED

a roll of varnish-insulated wire, 22- or 24-gauge

an iron nail, 10 cm (4 in.) long

electrical tape

a D-cell battery

paper clips

iron filings

a piece of paper

A note about safety

Be sure to disconnect your experiment from your batteries every time you're finished. Unattended batteries hooked up as described in the projects in this book can overheat or even explode. And never hook up your experiments to household power outlets or car batteries. Doing so will result in serious injury.

INSTRUCTIONS

1 Coil the wire around the nail at least 100 times, leaving loose ends at least 5 cm (2 in.) long. Cut wire to the length needed.

2 Tape each end of the wire to one of the battery terminals. You've just transformed a simple nail into an electromagnet.

3 Try to pick up some of the paper clips with the head or tip of your electromagnetized nail. How many can you pick up? What happens if you wind a length of wire around the nail 150 times? What about 200 times? Can you pick up more paper clips than before?

4 With 200 coils around the nail, position your electromagnet beneath a piece of paper and spread the iron filings on top of the paper. Tap the paper a few times, and you'll see the shape of an electromagnetic field emerge, much like the ones created by permanent magnets.

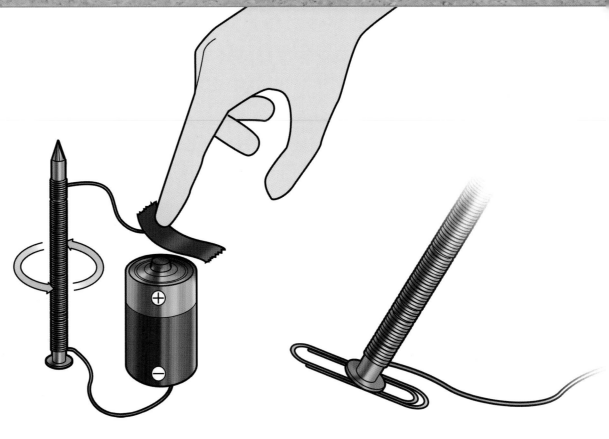

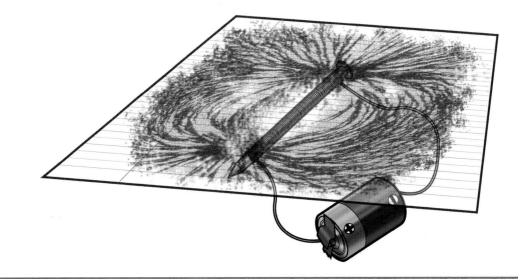

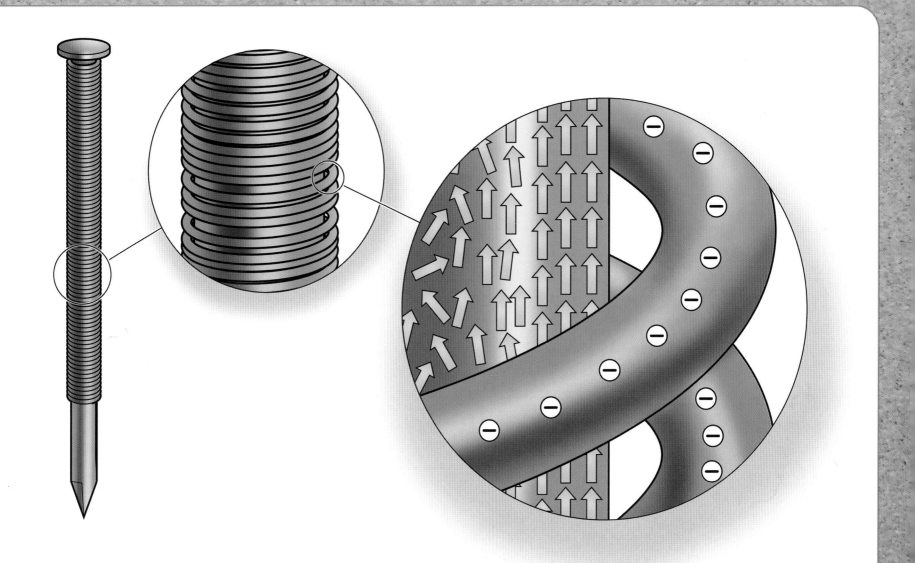

When you coil an electrified wire many times around something metal — say, an iron nail — the electrons running through the wire attract the iron in the nail, making the iron line up and point in one direction. This strengthens the electormagnetic field and transforms an ordinary nail into a magnet.

The simple magnetic field created in this experiment mirrors the idea behind a maglev rail system: When magnets on the track ahead of the train are "excited," they pull the train forward. At the same time, magnets behind the train alternate currents to push it along. It's sort of like dangling a high-powered carrot in front of a horse while swatting it from behind at the same time.

MAGLEV: THE TRAIN OF TOMORROW?

There are several ways to levitate an object with magnets: electromagnetically, electrodynamically and with permanent magnets.

Here's a look at how each stacks up:

Electromagnetic levitation:
This is the kind of maglev most often used in commercial trains today and those planned for the future. Electromagnetically levitated trains wrap around their tracks. Magnets on the underside of the track pull the train upward, so the train lifts off the top of the track. Electromagnetic trains can levitate and move forward under the power of electromagnets on the tracks.

Electrodynamic levitation:
Electromagnets on the tracks repel the magnets underneath the train, pushing the train up off the track. Electrodynamic maglevs can levitate but cannot propel themselves forward. To move ahead, such maglevs need a second system — such as motors mounted on the tracks — to push the train forward.

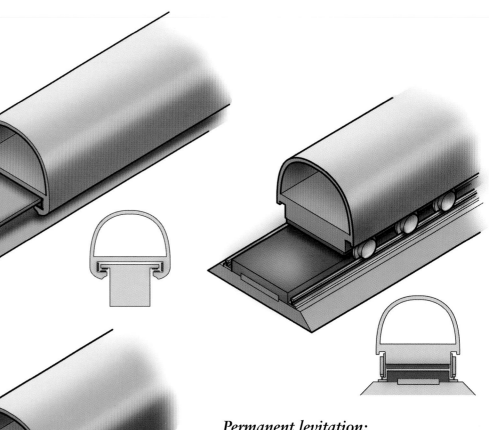

Permanent levitation:
A new design called the Inductrack system has been developed to use permanent magnets to levitate a train at low speeds. So far, this fridge-magnet-on-steroids design can only manage 5 km/h (3 m.p.h.), but NASA has started funding research to see if the technology could someday be used to launch satellites.

Magnet tracks and other uses

Electromagnets have also been used in particle accelerators to try to discover more about the origins of the universe. Examples of this are the Large Hadron Collider at the European Organization for Nuclear Research (CERN) and the synchrotrons that act as giant microscopes, such as the one in Saskatoon, Canada. Both use groups of amazingly strong electromagnets, arranged in a giant ring, to accelerate particles close to the speed of light. In doing so, these railways of light may help unlock the secrets of how the universe was formed.

Electromagnets can also be used in battle as experimental high-speed, high-power weapons, such as "rail guns," and in propelling objects into space. To the average person, though, electromagnets will likely become most useful in high-speed transportation systems: in other words, trains.

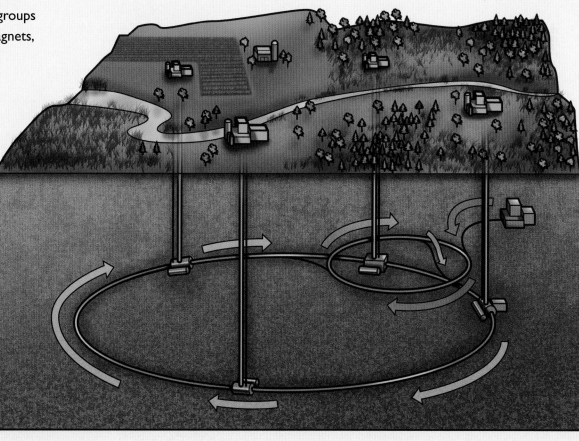

The Large Hadron Collider was built in a tunnel about 100 m (330 ft.) underground, near Geneva, Switzerland. Using superconducting magnets, it spreads Earth's smallest known particles in a giant ring at close to the speed of light.

Ride a real maglev

Built by a German company, the Shanghai maglev is one of the few real maglevs in commercial use today. This 30 km (19 mi.) line looks a bit like the futuristic monorails at large theme parks. It connects an airport in Shanghai, China, to one of the city's outer suburbs. The train has a standard cruising speed of about 430 km/h (267 m.p.h.), with a maximum speed of close to 500 km/h (310 m.p.h.).

The Shanghai maglev works by electromagnetic levitation. Its electromagnets, attached to the train's undercarriage, are attracted toward stator packs on the guideway's underside. This "pulls" the train up, levitating it to just less than 1 cm (1/2 in.) from the guideway's underside and roughly 15 cm (6 in.) above the guideway. (The train remains levitated even when it's not moving.) Other guidance magnets in the train's body keep it horizontally stable and centered along the track during travel.

Project #4: MAKE A MAGLEV TEST TRACK

By repeating the build of the magnetic field experiment earlier in the book (see page 25), you can create a model maglev track with a miniature "train." This setup, or array, of electromagnets mimics the effect of the real coils and wires found along a full-scale maglev track.

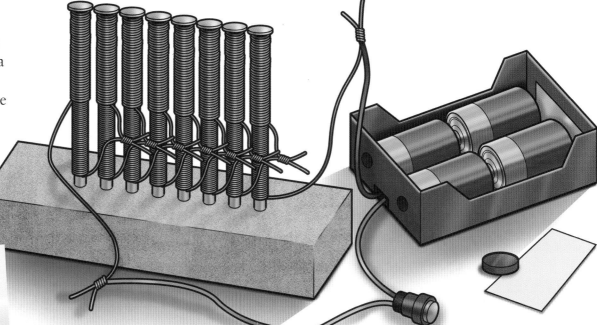

YOU WILL NEED

a small disk magnet

white glue

10 cm (4 in.) strip of paper

electrical tape

8 or more iron nails

50 m (164 ft.) varnish-insulated wire, 22- or 24-gauge

sandpaper

an electric drill (optional; see train-building tip on page 32)

a block of Styrofoam

4 D-cell batteries

a battery holder to accommodate 4 D-cell batteries

a simple push-button on/off switch

Expert interview

"Watch how softly your magnet hovers over your homemade 'track.' I'm always amazed at how smooth the ride is when I step on a maglev train. Generally, the force you feel when the train gets moving is gradual, about 0.1 G. Because of this, riding on a maglev like the one in Shanghai feels less like a train and more like being on a passenger jet at cruising altitude."

— Laurence Blow, President, MaglevTransport, Inc.

INSTRUCTIONS

1 Glue the magnet to the paper and set aside to dry. (The strip of paper is used to guide the magnet over the "track.")

2 Assemble eight electromagnets (like the one created in project #3) by tightly coiling wire up each nail and halfway back down. Leave 2.5 cm (1 in.) at the point of the nail bare, and leave at least 5 cm (2 in.) of wire free at each end. Sand the varnish off each wire end.

3 Plunge each nail–wire assembly into the Styrofoam. The nails should stand in a straight line, close enough so that their heads almost touch. Twist together the top wire on the first nail and the bottom wire of the nail next door. Apart from their wires, the nails should not touch. Once you have connected each nail with its neighbor in this way, there should be one free wire at the beginning of the track and one at the end.

Train-building tip

To quickly wind wire around a nail, place the nail in the chuck of an electric drill. Tape one end of the wire near the tip of the nail, and with an adult's help, carefully wind the wire up the whole nail, then back halfway, guiding it with your hand.

4 Twist the free wire at the beginning of the track with one of the two battery-holder wires. Connect the other battery-holder wire to one of the push-button prongs. Then connect the free wire at the other end of the track to the other push-button prong.

5 Fit four D-cell batteries together in the battery holder. Switch on the power and hold the magnet above the track, using the paper to guide the magnet back and forth as it floats. Be careful not to let your magnet slip off the track. A derailment here is a constant possibility. No pressure! Just imagine the challenges of keeping a real train on track …

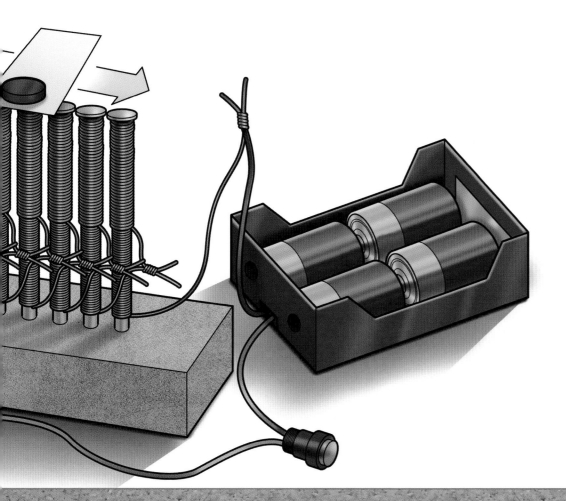

In this basic model, a simple push-button switch controls when your track is turned on to levitate. In a full-scale electromagnetic track, computers control when a train levitates and by how much. They also keep the train balanced as it glides over the electromagnets. Think of how many calculations per second a real maglev rail system must have to make in order to give passengers a fast, safe ride!

TRAINS OF THE FUTURE

Although this "futuristic" mode of transportation has been around for more than 30 years, maglev technology remains unperfected. Maglev trains take much of their trips to accelerate to top speed and then decelerate; they require constant computer monitoring to stay afloat; and most models are fairly vulnerable to wind shear (changes in wind speed or direction). In addition, maglev track is among the most expensive on Earth to construct.

On the other hand, several maglevs have been in commercial use and many countries plan to build more. As traditional fossil fuels become harder to get, electric and electromagnetic trains will become more cost effective for short- to medium-haul trips.

Countries around the world are considering plans for maglev and high-speed electric trains on conventional tracks. In Brazil, researchers are working on a maglev "cobra" model that uses many short, stubby cars to get around tight turns without having to slow down. Scientists propose such a rail system could be built to link the major cities of Rio de Janeiro and São Paulo before Brazil hosts World Cup soccer in 2014.

And if you think it would be fun to ride on a super-fast train at hundreds of kilometers (miles) an hour, how about riding an ultra-fast maglev at thousands of kilometers (miles) an hour … through a vacuum! At a top speed of 6000 km/h (3728 m.p.h.), travelers could journey across the ocean in about 55 minutes!

Possible? Researchers at the Massachusetts Institute of Technology (MIT) say maybe someday, if you put the vacuum tunnel underwater. That's because a train traveling through a vacuum — like the kind you find in space — wouldn't encounter any air friction. That would make it free to travel as fast as an electrical current allows. Putting the tube underwater would keep the train out of the way of other vehicles or damaging weather.

Though such a setup would cost as much as a human mission to Mars, Professor Ernst Frankel at MIT says an underwater tunnel connecting Boston and New York City along the eastern seaboard could be a realistic test of such technology. Instead of a four-hour train ride between these cities, Dr. Frankel estimates that a maglev in a near-vacuum tunnel could make the trip in 45 minutes. (That's even less time than an airplane trip between the two cities.)

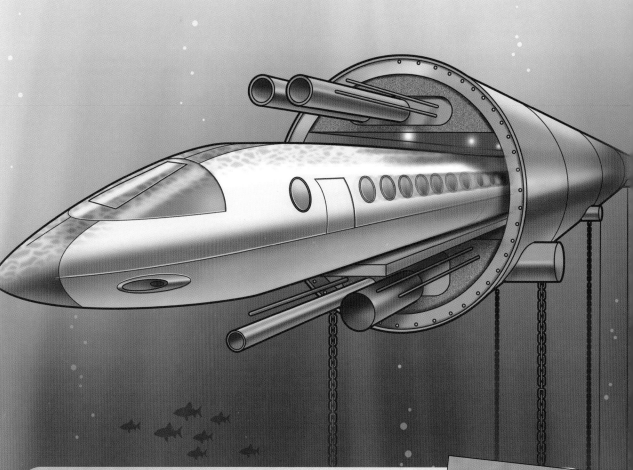

Expert interview

"Though you can't ride a supersonic maglev train under the ocean today, I can tell you that this kind of train already exists: At the Massachusetts Institute of Technology, we've shot small model-sized 'trains' through test tunnels at more than 1000 km/h (621 m.p.h.). Imagine the online model mentioned at the end of this book with no air to slow it down."
— MIT Professor Emeritus Ernst Frankel

TRAINS OF THE *DISTANT* FUTURE

Think the idea of underwater magnet trains is far out? Try maglevs in space! Believe it or not, NASA is exploring the idea of using maglev technology to launch satellites into space: The idea is that a satellite would ride a maglev "sled" along a giant launch ring that ends in a ramp. A rocket attached to the sled would leave the ramp and scream through the atmosphere at 23 times the speed of sound — nearly 30 000 km/h (19 000 m.p.h.)!

Other extreme uses of next-generation trains include maglevs on the Moon or even Mars — not as subways or railway systems (things already float pretty well there), but to launch equipment and people out and away to even farther places in the solar system.

It all sounds like something in the distant future, but it's amazing how quickly "the future" becomes the present. What's almost certain is that the people who will build these machines are the kids of today — in other words, you.

Will you have what it takes to dream up the trips of tomorrow? See you on the tracks!

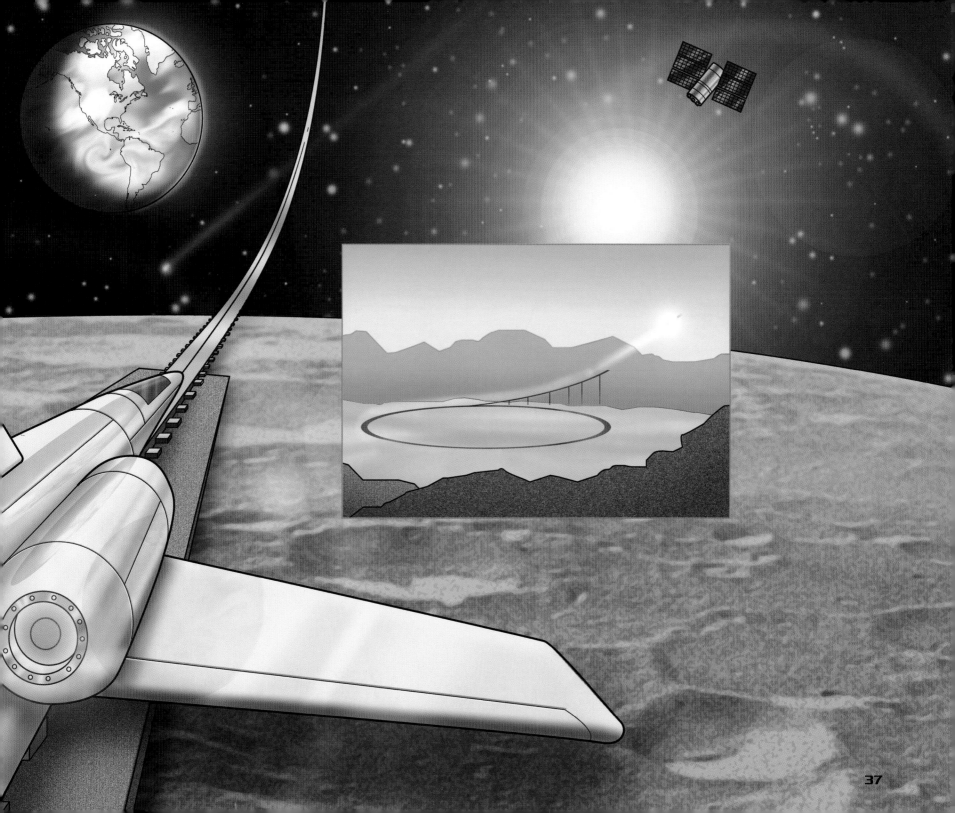

Project #5: MAKE A WORKING MAGLEV MODEL

Online Exclusive!

Don't live in Shanghai and can't wait another 10 years to see a maglev in operation? Enlist a group of friends — or even your whole class — to make a working maglev model with an armload of items found in most hardware stores.

This maglev model accurately reproduces the array of magnets used in Shanghai's maglev system. Find the full plans — along with demo images and video — online at **www.kidscanpress.com/machinesofthefuture**

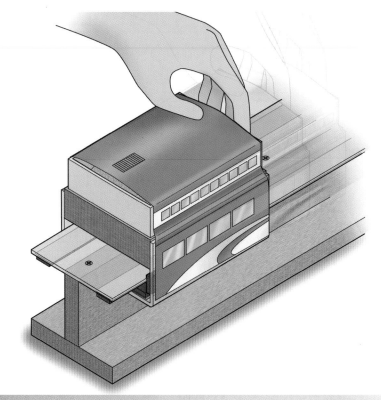

YOU WILL NEED

1 m (3 ft.) of one-by-six lumber, planed

1 m (3 ft.) of one-by-four lumber, planed

1 strip of clear Lexan (polycarbonate), 7 cm x 90 cm (2-3/4 in. x 35 in.)

an electric drill with a countersink bit

nine 2.5 cm (1 in.) wood screws with flat heads

fifteen 2.5 cm (1 in.) brass wood screws with flat heads

a roll of double-sided tape

approximately eighty-six 2.5 cm (1 in.) long latch magnets

2 rectangles of Lexan (polycarbonate), 7 cm x 10 cm (2-3/4 in. x 4 in.)

small, wide plastic container, sand

scraps of balsa wood, corrugated plastic board or another flat, smooth material

Expert interview

"Maglev trains in use today use computers to turn electromagnetic fields on and off in the right order, many times a second in the vehicle or along the tracks. In this model, you can do the same thing without computers by adding and subtracting weights until your model hovers above the rails you'll construct. Believe it or not, the air gap between a real-life maglev and its tracks is 6 to 10 mm (1/2 to 3/8 in.). Your model may have just a small fraction of that gap and still be able to 'levitate.'"
— Laurence Blow, President, MaglevTransport, Inc.

Glossary

Accelerate: To increase the speed of an object.

Biodiesel: A type of fuel based on renewable resources (such as soybean oil) or waste resources (such as leftover cooking fat from restaurants).

Bullet train: The fastest of all high-speed passenger trains, usually powered by electricity. Bullet trains travel at 200–350 km/h (124–220 m.p.h.) or more and close to 600 km/h (370 m.p.h.) in test runs.

Cruising speed: The rate of motion that an object or vehicle can sustain for a long period of time.

Cylinder: A tube-shaped chamber in which the pressure of a gas or liquid moves a sliding piston.

Decelerate: To decrease the speed of an object.

Diesel: A type of fuel designed for diesel engines. Often a fossil fuel.

Electricity: Electric current used as a source of power.

Electromagnet: A magnet made by passing an electric current through coils of wire.

Energy efficiency: The amount of energy required to accomplish a task with a minimum of time and effort. The more energy efficient something is, the less energy it wastes.

Fossil fuel: Any organic material, such as oil, coal or natural gas, that can catch fire and burn, and that comes from the remains of ancient life.

Freight train: A railroad train made up of freight cars, carrying cargo.

Guideway: A structure (usually made of concrete) used to support and guide trains that ride over it.

High-speed train: A type of passenger train that travels significantly faster than the normal speed of rail traffic — 150–200 km/h (90–124 m.p.h.) or more.

Hovercraft: A vehicle that can move over water or land on a cushion of air.

Levitation: The act of causing an object to rise into the air and float, defying gravity.

Locomotive: A self-propelled vehicle that serves as an engine to pull (and sometimes push) a train or individual railroad cars.

Monorail: A single-rail track for vehicles traveling on it or suspended from it.

Passenger train: A railroad train made up of passenger cars carrying people.

Piston: A disk or cylinder-shaped part tightly fitting and moving inside a cylinder.

Rail: A guide or pair of guides that provide a running surface for the wheels of trains.

Signal: A sign that can change to tell train operators what speed to travel, which direction switches are set, or any other conditions on the tracks.

Top speed: The fastest rate of motion at which an object or vehicle can travel.

Spike: A gigantic nail used for fastening together pieces of traditional railroad track.

Stator pack: An electromagnet or group of electromagnets that provide motion for vehicles, such as maglev rail systems.

Switch: A track structure for diverting moving trains from one track to another. Switches are usually a set of movable rails.

Wheel: A circular frame or disk that revolves on an axis to help move vehicles such as trains along a track.

Undercarriage: The supporting framework underneath a vehicle. A train's undercarriage is where the wheels, suspension and other parts that connect to the track are fitted.

Vacuum: A space with absolutely no matter, such as parts of deep space. Vehicles can travel through an artificial vacuum faster than they travel through air on Earth.

Index